Table Of Conte...

M000170398

Introduction

Let me start by first comparing myself to Brad Pitt.

Hey, stop laughing long enough for me to clarify that. What I mean is, I'm comparing myself to Brad Pitt who played the role of Billy Beane, General Manager of the Oakland Athletics in one of my favorite movies, "Moneyball." So I guess it's more accurate for me to say I'm comparing myself to Billy Beane.

Most people would say "Moneyball" was a movie about baseball. I don't necessarily agree. I saw it as a movie about a revolutionary business model.

Billy Beane looked at baseball through a different lens than everybody else; and they all thought he was nuts.

They played the game the same way it had been played since it was first invented.

How was Billy Beane's method different? He understood the power of numbers. Unlike everybody else, he realized that the game ultimately came down to numbers and statistics. By understanding the numbers better than anybody else, he changed the game forever. But he didn't just change the way the game was played, he changed the way the game was won. He was a visionary who opened everybody's eyes, and today everybody follows Billy Beane's model because it works.

Today, I help people look at real estate through a different lens than just about anyone else. I'm helping smart investors think differently about how they've done things the same way over and over. I show them how to dig deep into the numbers and find money to be made. Most investors don't know this, most investors don't do this. There's a lot more meat on the bone than most investors realize. And that's what we are talking about, so get ready. We're the "Moneyball Guys" of real estate investing. That's what a deal architect is—he looks at each deal through a different lens than everybody else. I won't try to get you to stop what you're doing well. I'll encourage you to keep doing what is working with your wholesaling or fix-n-flipping... but I will show you things you can easily add to the business you're already doing to make it a whole new ball game! A more successful and profitable ball game (aka business)!

In a strong economy, some factors shrink the profit margins for real estate investors. Buy low / sell high is a tough sell. We're flooded with guru seminar graduates and all the HGTV watchers who are Chip and Joanna wannabes. They're running around making discount cash offers on properties. This means your offers have to be smarter than theirs.

Competition has never been stronger, however, there's a portion of real investing you can play that most other investors can't. And it puts you way ahead of the game. Creative Financing!

There are three other big challenges that investors face:
- The seller won't budge on their price because they're not desperate to sell.
- The seller owes too much on his mortgage so he can't take a low price.
- There's something weird or unique about the property that will make it hard for you to resell.

In this book, I'll explain how creative financing can make these obstacles go away. These techniques help wholesalers double conversion rates on the offers made because we can now control three important factors:
- The terms of the sale.
- The terms of the loan.
- The terms of the agreement.

I've spent four decades coaching investors in their creative financing and note businesses. I have personally bought over 40,000 deals myself—the majority of which were buying notes from professional REIs. The rest were from individual "mom and pops" who carried only one seller-financed note their entire life. Trust me, I have learned some "Moneyball" lessons in these deals. This combination of experiences are what led me to perfecting this strategy.

I know what REIs need and what mom and pops will accept. It made me realize that I had a seat with a vantage point that literally no one else in the country had sat in (at least to the degree I had been there). If experience matters, this lifetime of customers and their notes has led me to a unique place on the horizon. I've learned what separates successful real estate buyers from all the rest.

What makes them more successful is that they understand the numbers better than the other guy, so the offers they make are smarter than the offers the other guy makes. About ten to fifteen percent of the best investors say they "do creative financing" and buy on "terms" offers. They'll also say, "Hey, I know how to make offers with seller financing."

Most of these guys only know how to make offers with one variable, maybe two, and if that doesn't work they've got no backup plan. But one variable doesn't make it creative. On the other hand (the hand with the money in it), the smart guys know how to look deeply into the numbers of every deal because they understand creative financing gives you about forty variables in your tool belt to work with.

It's like the smart buyers are playing Major League Baseball and the other guys are stuck in Little League. They're both playing the same game but at totally different skill levels, and the Little Leaguers don't even know what they don't know. But once they learn, they hit it out of the park! So, how do you make smarter offers?

You need to understand all the tools available in the creative financing toolbox. Lots of buyers know about a tool or two, so they think they know all they need to know. (They're the buyers whose offers are ending up in the trash can.) Or they don't try to make an offer on a property because the seller's low equity tells them that a discounted price will never be accepted since it's not enough to pay off their mortgage.

The other day I was plugging in a lamp and the nearest socket was several feet away. So I stretched the cord as far as it would go, but it was about six inches too short. I had to laugh because all I needed was a six-inch extension cord!

That's when the lightbulb went on. (In my head—not the one in the lamp.) That little six-inch extension cord that I needed to bridge the gap between the plug and the socket is a lot like how creative financing can bridge the gap between a rejected deal and a done deal. It's how you, the buyer, can connect with a seller when you can't quite agree on the price.

The vast majority of discounted cash offers that real estate investors make to buy a property end up in the trash can (they get rejected)—especially in today's market when sellers are holding out for every dime. On most deals today, the "asking" price has become the "insisting" price. Today's rejection rate is around 95% because investors are bidding below the asking price.

You can't play Moneyball with a batting average like this. But just like my lamp cord, a whole bunch of those rejected offers fall just a tiny bit short of what the buyer is insisting on—sometimes by only a few thousand bucks.

CHAPTER ONE

BE A SMARTER INVESTOR
By Bridging The Price Gap

The average investor would assume there was no way to make the deal happen, then move on to making more offers on more properties and keep getting more of the same result (rejected offers).

The smart investor understands that great numbers in one category can more than make up for less-than-great numbers in another category (like the purchase price).

The smart investor digs deep into the numbers to use creative financing that turns trash into cash. It allows you to reach into your trash can full of rejected offers and turn several handfuls into done deals. I like this visual, since you're reading this, I assume you do too. Lots of sellers have a firm selling price cemented in their mind. If an offer doesn't match their price, it goes straight into the trash can. But even when a seller is as stubborn as a mule on the asking price, they can be surprisingly flexible on how and when they get their money. If you know how to put together smart offers and present it in a way that shows the seller how it meets their needs and possibly exceeds their desires, you'll be closing plenty of deals.

Never forget that seller financing is not just for when you're the seller. Knowing how to creatively architect a deal in your favor when you're the buyer is what separates the grown-ups from the rugrats in real estate investing.

Here's an example. Meet Kevin, he is one of our young NoteSchool alums who lives in Seattle. He's really a smart guy and he's getting married soon to a really lucky lady. He had a brilliant plan for buying a duplex to live in.

He and his future bride could live in one side and rent the other. That way his whole mortgage payment would be covered by the rental income from the other half.

So he and his fiancé looked at duplexes on the market and found the one they liked. The selling price was not his initial focus. That may seem a little weird, but it's how a deal architect thinks, I'll get you there. It was a model that allowed him to live payment free, and by the way, he only wanted to start with a cash down payment of $5,000. Crazy or smart?

I'm going with smart ;-)

He knew that the future rent payments from his tenant would be covering his monthly mortgage payment. He carefully worked out the cash flow model beginning with how much he could expect to bring in from rent. Then he used that number to determine what his maximum monthly payment would be. He concluded that the rent payments would cover a mortgage for a purchase price of $265K.

He found a property where the seller owned the property free and clear and was willing to carry seller financing, even accept his low down payment. But the seller was asking $325K, above what he calculated he could pay to stay within his money rules.

Kevin floated the idea of seller financing to the seller, and they were open to the idea, but the guy insisted the interest rate be 5% which jeopardized Kevin's ability to live in his side for free. (The typical REI that only knew to pitch 0% never would have gotten to first base.) So Kevin crafted 5% interest into the offer and made his pitch for $265K. But, the seller said no because his $325K asking price was etched in stone.

Just like with most deals (and just like my lamp cord), there was a gap between what he wanted to pay and what the buyer would take. For Kevin to make this deal work, he would have to craft a one-of-a-kind offer to fit the needs of the deal, rather than trying to squeeze the deal into the mold of a one-size-fits-all offer that less savvy buyers make on every deal.

He went through the numbers on paper. He could make a $5K down payment, then seller finance the other $260K at 5% for 30 years. But he was still 60 grand short on meeting their $325K asking price. Kevin is no rookie, and he was already at a deeper thinking level than most, but he just didn't see a way to fix the deal. The resistance factor was so high that he was about to assign the deal to the trash can and move on. But then he did another smart thing.

He called me! I've been doing creative financing since I was 20, so I've learned how to bridge the gap that saved tons of deals.

I took a long hard look at the numbers and told him to make one more suggestion to the seller to bridge their $60K problem. I said to give them their full asking price, put $5K down, and finance the first $260K at 5% like the seller was adamant on; but to ask the seller if they would put the remaining $60K on a separate note from the first $260K.

I told him how to position the counter when he served it up. I told him to ask that the terms on this second note be 0%, with no payments until the full amount is due in 15 years. I said, "I'll betcha they'll take your counter if you say it right." He questioned my confidence they'd accept but did as I asked.

My last piece of advice was don't stutter, keep a straight face and assume they will agree when he made the offer because it was so heavily in his favor. This is how you play Moneyball.

Always remember: The art of architecting a deal is not simply knowing how to run the math—it's knowing how to dictate the terms and "sell it". Too many math nerds underestimate the value of people skills.

Kevin took my advice and re-pitched his offer. He asked the seller to finance the second $60K note at 0%. But he lost a little of his nerve and said it would be due in 10 years instead of 15. But hey, I'll still let him hang out with me.

How'd it all shake out? The seller said YES, so now it's a done deal rescued from the trash can thanks to creative financing. He's living in his new duplex and renting out the other half to cover his monthly payment.

Creativity. You gotta love it!

Think about the offers you made last month that went nowhere. On some of them, you and the seller were probably miles apart. But how many of your offers got rejected even though you and the seller were only a few thousand dollars apart? My guess is it was probably several of them. Now imagine if you could have bridged that gap with creative financing and closed two or three or four of those extra deals last month. Now multiply that times twelve and think about how much more money you could have made last year by playing Moneyball like Kevin!

I walk through deals exactly like Kevin's where you can see step-by-step how we lay them out at **NoteSchoolTraining.com**. Join me and see how we break down deals so you can see the best way to structure offers to create long term wealth.

CHAPTER TWO

BE A SMARTER INVESTOR
By Negotiating The Terms

Lately, my phone has been ringin' off the hook. I keep getting call after call after call on the same topic. Lots of these calls come from mega-seasoned real estate investors. Even though these are top-level investors who buy 50 to 200 houses a year, they're having some serious challenges.

I'm hearing the same story over and over and over, just like a broken record: "Eddie, wholesaling and flippin' ain't working as well as they used to. Two things are happening; first sellers won't sell with a discounted price, or when I'm offering my advanced creative financing where I'm buying a property and suggesting a seller-financed loan at the interest rate I want, the seller walks."

That's why I've been working like never before to open up people's minds so they can play Moneyball instead of Lowball. They could be converting more deals by using the full array of tools available with creative financing to put money in their pockets.

You can't succeed in real estate if all you do is make lowball cash offers on every property. A few years ago, I didn't even attempt to explain creative seller financing to my ninja real estate pals because they were having such success wholesaling houses they thought adding something would be stupid. Well, that was then. Now they're spending more on marketing but getting fewer results, and wholesaling is not as successful. They're coming to me and they're listening harder than ever before. I'm showing them the secret sauce they didn't know existed, and they're lovin' it! Once we take them through the process, the "Wows" are 100%.

The problem with most of their current seller financed offers is that they all have the same percentage rate stuck in their head: Zero, even for the most innovative investors who know something about creative finance. Now that's not very creative. Lots of real estate gurus have everybody thinking you gotta get 0% to make a profit. Everybody has zeroes stuck in their head! I open the minds of real estate investors to show there's a whole lot more to sellerfinancing than just offering 0% interest. It's great when you can get a seller to finance the property for 0% interest, but I only see it happen about 20% of the time. When the seller won't bite on 0%, all is not lost. Not by a longshot.

The interest rate is only one of about fifty points I show you to architect a deal if you know what you're doing, and most investors don't. Learn the whole toolbox of techniques and you'll have the upper hand over competitors making offers on the same properties.

Even though you may not be getting the numbers you want for the price or interest rate, you can still architect a killer deal with numbers in your favor from other categories that will earn a healthy profit. A Money Baller in our industry knows other ways to create an equally good deal! There are many, many ways to structure the deal you want other than offering all with financing at 0%. Remember our friend Kevin in Seattle?

Never forget that a seller-financed deal (even with a higher percentage rate than you want to pay) will still give you the edge over a bank loan. You have to be knowledgeable, creative, and flexible—which gives you advantages over a loan at the bank or a cash buy.

Your first advantage in qualifying for a loan is the time factor required.
The bank demands your work history, credit history, tax returns, and blah, blah, blah. But the seller makes you do absolutely nothing. You may not believe this, but it's true: In my career, I've reviewed 300,000 to 400,000 notes; and among mom & pop seller financed notes, only 1 in 500 pulled a credit report on the buyer! This avoids a huge hassle factor to make your deal come together faster instead of waiting for the bank to plow through their stack of paperwork.

The reason the bank gathers all that information is that they're going to make you personally guarantee the loan, which leads to the second advantage. The seller who is financing your deal won't insist you do a personal guarantee as the bank does. (Even though I used to sign loans with a bank for 5 or 10 million dollars, after doing these deals for four decades I don't do that anymore. Those days are behind me.)

Your third advantage is the down payment amount. We structure deals consistently with zero down payment. There's a myriad of ways to get the seller money at closing, but it doesn't have to be down payment money. And I've got the case studies that explain it all. Sound good so far?

If the seller gets the price and interest rate they want, sometimes they'll say OK to zero down. (Good luck finding a bank that approves your loan with a zero down payment. And if you can find a hard money lender that will accept zero down, they're gonna stick it to you with a high rate that won't work for long term financing.) Even if the seller insists on 20% down, **they don't insist that it be your money!** I can show you twenty creative strategies used in real- life case studies that demonstrate how you can avoid putting up your own money.

Advantage four is the first payment due date. The bank will insist on the first payment 30 days after closing. But with seller financing, I can push the first payment to three years down the road, and I've done it numerous times.

The fifth advantage of seller financing over the bank is the exchange or release of property as their collateral. The bank's probably never going to release their collateral 'til they get all their money, but I can give case study after case study where the seller was far more flexible. What if you buy a property and then release part but not all of the collateral at closing? Or let you move the "favorable terms" loan to a completely different property. You might move the loan on Property A to Property B, which releases Property A. Or you buy a property and then release part but not all of the collateral at closing. I can give you lots more examples. That is exactly what I do in the live training I give. I walk through examples so you can understand and see live how many opportunities you have. Go to *NoteSchoolTraining.com* to register.

Those are just five points of the negotiation toolbox, with the sixth being the interest rate... and there are dozens more.

When you negotiate with any seller, you have to present your terms correctly and tactfully—what I call the "talk-off." If you don't serve it up right, the seller won't agree to squat. How to dictate the terms and present it skillfully is part of the art of deal-making. Just like any skill, the more you do it the better you get.

Right now, most investors close one deal out of twenty offers. That's a 5% success rate (and a 95% failure rate). By learning the whole toolbox of seller financing techniques, you can double or triple your success rate. It's game changing!

Let me ask you a question. If you could get a loan for $20 to $50 million dollars with no lender qualifications, no guarantee to the lender, and you could dictate the terms to your lender so that they are way below traditional financing, are you in?

Speaking of dictating the terms, if you were in a banker's office right now applying for a loan, and you could dictate pretty much whatever terms you wanted, what would your ideal terms include? If you like how that sounds, you're ready to learn how to play Moneyball!

We play Moneyball at **NoteSchoolTraining.com**, join us!

CHAPTER THREE

BE A SMARTER INVESTOR
By Being Flexible On Price

Mike Tyson said, "Everybody's got a plan until they get punched in the mouth." Real estate investors used to be able to make a Lowball offer on a house, then either wholesale them or fix it up, then flip either way for a big profit. They were buying at a wholesale price then selling at a retail price.

Now that's how the game used to be played. In a buyer's market lots of people make incredible transactional income. That's still not getting rich but it was a super high paying salary. If your plan to succeed in today's market is to Lowball every offer, you just got punched in the mouth. See all those little white things scattered on the floor? Those are your teeth.

So when the seller won't or can't accept the discount, I'm saving people's teeth by showing them how to switch from playing Lowball to Moneyball.

Buying a property at a wholesale price and selling at a retail price, or fixing it up to resell for a huge profit is how things used to be, but it ain't the way things are moving. Today's sellers are not only tossing most of the lowball offers into the trash, but they're also tossing anything that doesn't match their full asking price into the trash. Investors are having to make offers on twenty different properties for every one deal that goes through.

That's a 5% success rate and a 95% failure rate. City landfills are overflowing with real estate offers that never became deals!

Investors and house flippers talk to me all the time to complain about a lack of inventory even though they've doubled their marketing costs to get leads. They're frustrated that they can't find inventory at the low, wholesale prices they used to pay. But I tell them it's not a lack of inventory––it's a lack of people saying, "Yes, I'll accept the offer you put on the table because it's better than the other nineteen I got." When you double or triple that 5% success rate, you've increased your success exponentially. You might still close one deal out of twenty the old traditional way with a low cash offer, but with a certain degree of creativity, it's not out of the realm of possibilities that you might close two more deals on top of that *my way.* You need to learn the art of architecting a seller-financed deal on a property where you buy at a **retail price,** but structured with **wholesale terms** that are heavily in your favor as the buyer.

As crazy as this may sound, yes, you can still make money when you pay the full retail price… IF you know how to buy on wholesale terms and not just the price. Too many buyers only negotiate the price but know very little about negotiating the **wholesale terms!** And if a person is coachable, I'm happy to be their coach and explain it all. This is what I love doing!

Some years it's a buyer's market, and some years it's a seller's market, **but every year is a negotiator's market!** There are all kinds of ways to carve it up and still close a killer deal. For example, instead of getting a one-time check for transactional income, you could get your check plus twenty or thirty more years of checks on top of that.

Never forget that there are three ways to dictate to the seller on any deal:
- Terms of the sale.
- Terms of the loan.
- Terms of the agreement (all the other loan documents).

As the deal architect, you're in charge of all three areas. If you were to resort to getting money from a bank or hard money lender, you can only control the price, and only if the seller agrees to it. You also lose control over the terms of the loan plus the terms of the agreement, which are the two most important aspects of the deal for transactional income and wealth-building potential. With creative financing, your deal doesn't use standard Fannie Mae documents with all the red tape. Imagine having the freedom to cross out all the things you don't like when the banker hands you some loan papers. As the deal architect, you take the lender's rules and throw 'em out the window because the seller is the lender and you're dictating the terms. Now that's fun!

When you have the training and knowledge to structure the financing to your advantage, and how to properly serve up your offer to the seller, you'll have a huge leg up on the nineteen other investors whose offers end up in the landfill because the buyer said yes to yours.

I hope you believe in planning, setting goals, and mapping out your strategy to grow your business. As you make your plans, remember this. One of the most important investments many investors overlook is the priority of investing in *yourself.*

You need to keep learning and growing because the market keeps changing. Change is only scary to people who have stopped learning. So learn to love learning! A changing market will actually benefit the investor who keeps learning because he or she will be smarter than the investor still using tactics from three years ago.

Dogs graduate from *their* training, but investors never do! Continue your training at *NoteSchoolTraining.com.*

Take me for example. I'm an old dog that's still learning new tricks. After four decades and 40,000+ notes, I still learn as much as I can. As I map out the next several months, I'm attending several real estate events, plus other high-level masterminds with top people in real estate, where I'm the "Deal Architect for Creative Financing" who helps them do business mo' betta'. They invite me because creative financing is my thing and I show them how to bring creativity into their deals. I learn just as much from them in their areas of expertise as they learn from me in mine, which is what makes masterminds great. You learn solutions to problems you never knew you had! You get in the game you didn't even know existed. It makes me play at a whole new level.

We sponsor lots of events where investors can cross-pollinate and learn from each other's successes and failures because everybody participates and contributes. It's a great place to hear from other investors what it means to be a deal architect related to creative financing.

Life is full of twists, turns, and surprises, plus a whole lot of punches aimed right at your face. There's no way to predict how many times life will try to punch you in the mouth in the months ahead, but the smarter you are the more you learn to how to bob and weave.

I can tell you from experience, the punch you dodge feels a lot better than the punch that lands.

To see exactly what I am talking about, join me for a live training at **NoteSchoolTraining.com**.

CHAPTER FOUR

BE A SMARTER INVESTOR
By Knowing What's Possible

When a real estate investor learns how to structure deals with creative financing, it opens up a world of possibilities that other investors didn't even know existed. Where other investors only see roadblocks, brick walls, and landmines, a savvy investor sees a path to closing the deal. Here's a snippet of what you can do when your old Lowball game can't work so you upgrade your game to playing Moneyball.

In a typical market, a $150K house has a much lower chance of being bought for 70¢ on the dollar than an $80K house. And a $450K house has an even smaller chance than the $150K house. Expensive houses in this high asset class don't tend to get discounted like the lower asset class properties. There are two reasons for this. First, the sellers of expensive houses tend to be better off financially, so they're not as highly motivated to take your Lowball offer. Second, if they are highly motivated to sell because they can't afford their mortgage payment, they may have little or no equity in the property which means there's no way they can take your Lowball offer even if they wanted to. That's why the greater the asset class of the house, the greater the need is for creative financing.

I know I said this earlier, but it's worth repeating. There are three main reasons why deals fail and cause untrained investors to throw in the towel:
- The seller won't accept your price.
- The seller can't accept your 70¢ on the dollar offer because he has little or no equity and owes 90¢ on the dollar.
- The property you're buying doesn't fit the wholesale market you plan to sell it to.

Point number two (above) is critical here. What about the house you won't even go look at because they owe more than you could ever pay when buying houses at discounted prices? Yeah, that deal! That's a reason why the Lowball investor would simply give up and move on. But a seasoned investor with a tool belt full of creative financing techniques can still close a deal even if there's virtually no equity.This is where so many investors are losing profits they never knew existed. They don't know what they don't know and it's hurting them. I have the heart to show real estate investors, both large and small, how to convert a lead and make money not just today with transactional income, but also build wealth to have money flowing into your mailbox for many years to come.

There's so much more money to be made on your deals than most investors realize—if you know where to find it. Here are the numbers on a typical deal, as done by three different levels of investors, with three very different potential outcomes:

Rugrat Investor	Experienced Investor	Moneyball Investor
Asking: $130,000	Asking: $130,000	Asking: $130,000
Offer: $100,000	Offer: $120,000	Offer: $130,000
ARV: $175,000	ARV: $175,000	ARV: $175,000
Status: Rejected	Status: Accepted	Status: Accepted
Potential Profit: $0	Potential Profit: $55,000	Potential Profit: $145,000

Where did the extra $90,000 in profit come from for the Moneyball Investor over the Experienced Investor? It came from knowing how the game is played. That's the magic of real estate Moneyball, and you need to learn how to play it.

Deals often come with certain obstacles, so to make a deal happen with lots of obstacles you have to be able to wrap your head around wrap notes. If you're gonna play Moneyball, you gotta understand wrap notes because they're one of the most flexible tools in the creative financing toolbox.

What exactly is a wrap note, and why are they so useful?

Here's a simple way to explain it. I live in Texas, so I can't go very long without my Tex-Mex fix. I'll order a sizzling platter of fajitas, then load up a warm tortilla with some grilled chicken or steak, peppers, onions, cheddar cheese, sour cream, and guacamole. (I may have to cut this chapter short and go grab some!) Well, that tortilla holds everything together, and without it you'd have a big mess instead of a tasty meal. That tortilla is the same thing as a wrap note. The seller's unpaid existing underlying mortgage goes in the middle like the meat and onions, even his second mortgage can go in there, if he has one. Then we have a newly created wrap note where the new buyer of the property pays the real estate investor and in turn the real estate investor then pays the bank on the underlying mortgage(s).

Here's the benefit, the underlying money owed to the bank is at a lower rate than the money owed to real estate investor on the higher rate wrap note. The net effect is these terms as structured work greatly in the real estate investor's favor. They make money on the arbitrage (the difference between the two interest rates and P&I payments).

For example, the seller's original 4% Fannie Mae loan is in there, and now you're "re-lending" that same money where you're charging a new buyer 6.50% via your wrap note with them. So you make 2.5% on the bank's money.

It allows the seller to get out of a property where they have built up little if any equity while a super high-quality buyer that is not bankable gets to be a homeowner via the wrap note versus being relegated to being a tenant in landlord situation. A win-win for all parties. Wrap notes have saved thousands of my client's deals from the trash can, and once you listen to some of my case studies and learn how to structure wrap notes on your own, they can save your deals, too.

This also can produce transactional "up front" income plus mailbox money for thirty years, as well.

If you know what's possible, hardly anything is impossible. Think about all the properties you decided not to bid on because the sellers owed too much and didn't have enough equity to accept a discounted price. Now imagine yourself making 2.5% on top of the money all those sellers owed on all those properties. Hmmm. Now you're thinking like a Money Baller!

I told 'ya this would be a short chapter!

For more real life case studies & examples, join me at **NoteSchoolTraining.com**.

You can get a great deal even when you don't get a great price.

CHAPTER FIVE

BE A SMARTER INVESTOR
By Getting To Know Your Seller

And even though every deal **ends up** on paper, the truly great deals don't **start out** on paper—even when you're playing Moneyball.

When someone comes to me for advice on a deal, I don't ask them the numbers first. I first want to learn about the DNA of the seller. The place where most great deals happen is at the kitchen table. It's the perfect place to have a meaningful conversation with your seller to find out what matters most to them.

You might do 200 real estate deals a year, but they might do only one deal every ten years so they're understandably a bit nervous. They're more relaxed at their kitchen table than in a real estate office where they tend to have their guard up.

Your first conversation is not about numbers; it's about finding out what's most important to the person selling the property. Let them do most of the talking while you do most of the listening. After chatting with your seller, you'll learn what to negotiate for, and you'll be able to decide which sets of numbers in your offer are most important to the seller so your deal can come together.

As you sit around the table, things get real. You'll learn where their pain points are and what they need to move on with the next chapter in their life. You'll learn if they want to be closer to their grandkids, or if they want to buy an RV and tour the country, or maybe it's a property they inherited and don't want, or they need money for their kid's college, or if they're getting a divorce.

As much as you'll hear real estate experts talk about how to run the numbers, never forget the importance of good old fashioned people skills. It's a dying art that I'm determined to keep alive!

As real estate buyers, we can increase the price we pay if we get soft termsthrough seller financing. For example low interest, no interest, deferred payment, long term notes, plus all those different 40 or 50 points you can negotiate. It all comes back to what you can negotiate with the seller. That's what tells you how good of a deal you made. I call it "dictating the terms of the deal" to the seller.

Noteholders bring notes to my doorstep all the time to sell to me, so I get an inside look at hundreds of thousands of deals. I look over the terms of some of these deals and think, "Why did anybody agree to this?" Well, they agreed to it because the buyer listened to the seller and understood their pain points, knew which tools could be used to put the terms together. Then, they presented their offer in a way that enabled the seller to move on with the next chapter in their life.

A seller is seldom going to dictate the **terms** the way they dictate the **price,** so they're open to soft terms. People are naturally used to a bank dictating the terms to them instead of the other way around, so there's a lot less pushback.

I'll often ask a seller, "Why did you agree to one or two percent interest or no down payment?" And they'll say, "Well, the guy gave me what I wanted," which means the buyer did a good job of finding out their pain points, then customized a one-of-a-kind deal to be structured around meeting those needs.

How can you dictate the terms to the seller? I'll break it down into two steps.

Step 1: You have to have a good interview with the seller. That's where you learn what's most important to them. You have to use some discernment because at first, it'll sound like there's no room to negotiate. But you'll figure out how to peel off one or two essentials to focus on.

Once you know what the buyer really wants and needs, other than just their asking price, you'll know which creative finance tools you'll need later on in the negotiation process to put together an offer that the seller will accept.

When you know which tools to use, you can negotiate a great deal without having to negotiate a great price, which the seller is probably not going to budge on anyway. You can architect a seller-financed deal that gives them the *price* they want with the *terms* you want.

Step 2: Know what you're negotiating for. There are so many things to negotiate that you can get lost in the details and lose sight of the big picture.

As you put together a deal that meets the needs of the seller, you have to remind yourself what it is that you want to get out of the deal. It's easy to leave out important parts of the negotiation that benefit you if you don't know what you're negotiating for. I can show you lots of case studies where the investor *got* what he wanted because he *knew* what he wanted and *asked* for it.

Out of the fifty or so tools in your seller financing toolbox, you'll never need all fifty on every deal. But you will need fifteen or so on *every* deal. But which fifteen will they be? And what order will you present them in? That's why there's wisdom in knowing what you're negotiating for. If you try to bring out every tool you've got, then you'll just confuse your seller and scare them off.

Once you understand the pain points of the seller and why they want to sell their property, you'll be much better equipped at structuring a deal that meets their needs. And your own!

Other than price, how many of the 50 or so other things can you name that can also be negotiated in your favor? If you can only think of a handful, you need to learn how to play Moneyball!

Go to **NoteSchoolTraining.com** to discover how you can play Moneyball starting today!